He Descended
into Hell

He Descended
into Hell

A Christological Study of the Apostles' Creed
and Its Implication to Christian Teaching
and Preaching in Africa

ELIKANA ASHERI LOVA
and
ELIA SHABANI MLIGO

RESOURCE *Publications* · Eugene, Oregon

HE DESCENDED INTO HELL
A Christological Study of the Apostles' Creed and Its Implication to Christian Teaching and Preaching in Africa

Resource Publications
An Imprint of Wipf and Stock Publishers
199 W. 8th Ave., Suite 3
Eugene, OR 97401

www.wipfandstock.com

ISBN 13: 978-1-4982-0621-1

Manufactured in the U.S.A.

Contents

Foreword

Facts and Disagreements in Interpretations

THE DISCUSSION ABOUT THE descent clause from the Apostles' Creed presented in this book is a discussion about what is considered 'fact' and what people disagree with within a particular perspective.[1] When we speak of a perspective, we cannot avoid touching about the existing dichotomy between 'facts' and 'disagreements.' Facts are self-existent, which means they are there irrespective of disagreements. The disturbing question concerns about the existence of disagreements in the midst of facts: If facts so exist, why do people disagree? What makes a particular assertion about a so-conceived fact accepted by the majority? It follows from these questions that if a particular fact is not a fact to all people, then a fact is a fact because of some people's assumptions about it. This means that it is a fact to those people who hold similar assumptions about it.

Disagreement, in this case, is not a disagreement about the existing fact, but about the assumption about the fact. The literary critic Stanley E. Fish, in his book *Is there a Text in This Class?* aptly points it out: "disagreements must occur between those who hold (or are held by) different points of view, and what is at stake in the disagreement is the right to specify what the facts can thereafter

1. For more explanations about the notion of "perspective" see Mligo, *Symbolic Interactionism*, 1 – 6.

be said to be."[2] Moreover, Tyler Cowen and Robin Hanson in their article called "Are Disagreements Honest? further state: "Not only do people disagree; they often consider their disagreements to be about what is objectively true, rather than about how they each feel or use words. Furthermore, people often consider their disagreements to be honest, meaning that the disputants respect each other's relevant abilities, and consider each person's stated opinion to be his best estimate of the truth, given his information and effort."[3] In the statements above, Fish and Cowen and Hanson refer us to a 'point of view,' a 'perspective,' as being the underlying source of the existence of a particular fact. For Fish, for example, disagreements about a particular fact "cannot be resolved by reference to the facts, because facts emerge only in the context of some point of view."[4] In this case, according to Fish, "Disagreements are not settled by the facts, but are the means by which the facts are settled."[5]

What Fish and Cowen and Hanson posit in the above statements concerns about the interpretation of a 'fact'. Here, the context at which a fact is regarded a fact is very crucial. Since there are numerous points of view and numerous facts within a particular point of view, then disagreements cannot be resolved by only pointing to particular facts. Disagreements serve as means through which particular facts are well-interpreted in a particular point of view.

The question of interpretation of particular facts in a particular point of view is the question of persuasion. An interpretation of facts is persuasion because facts emerge in different shapes at every point of view. According to Fish, literary criticism is a place where the act of persuasion is more explicit. It is a place "where everyone's claim is that his [or her] interpretation more perfectly accords with the facts, but where everyone's purpose is to persuade the rest of us to the version of the fact he [or she] espouses by

2. Fish, *Is there a Text in This Class?* 338.
3. Cowen & Hanson, "Are Disagreements Honest," (2001).
4. Fish, *Is There a Text in this Class?* 338.
5. Ibid.

persuading us to the interpretive principles in the light of which those facts will seem indisputable."[6] Therefore, the various interpretations of the descent clause discussed in this book are attempts at persuading people to agree with the validity of the clause in the Apostles' Creed.

But, what then does this book do with the clause? Does it present facts about it? Or, does it present disagreements about it? The argument of the book is vivid: to persuade people about the danger of the various interpretations of the descent clause to our current assumptions and contexts. Fish further states: "text, context and interpretation all emerge together." Since the three aspects emerge together, then there is a possibility for one interpretation to win over another. "It follows, then that when one interpretation wins out over another, it is not because the first has been shown to be in accordance with the facts but because it is from the perspective of its assumptions that the facts are now being specified. It is these assumptions, and not the facts they make possible, that are at stake in any critical dispute."[7] The various interpretations of the clause presented in this book are texts that had their own interpreters, their own contexts, their own persuasive purposes in regard to particular existing assumptions, within a particular point of view. The perspectives of their assumptions are the ones that most likely made them acceptable in their contexts of interpretation. What is mainly done by the authors of this book is to show that the context of interpretation has now changed; current interpreters hold different assumptions and have their own point of view. This change means that what was held as fact in regard to the descent can hardly be fact any more to those of current assumptions, context and point of view.

For example, I myself am inclined to reject the idea of immortality of souls implied by the descent doctrine which has been embraced by some denominations of the church for centuries. This disagreement follows my own Christian interpretation of death and the life hereafter. There are three reasons to the disagreement:

6. Ibid., 339.

7 Ibid

first, according to Scriptural utterance (1 Timothy 6: 16 cf. 1 Corinthians 15: 53) God alone has immortality. A human being has not been equal with God since creation; a human being was not equal to God since creation, is still not, and will never be. To consider the soul of man as being immortal is to equate it with God who created it, hence blaspheming.

Second, it should be clearly understood that sin originated not in the body but in the soul of man. In this case, therefore, the soul stands primarily, and above all, under the judgment of death together with the body.

Third, it should be clearly known also that the being of man is a psychosomatic (soul and body) unity (Genesis 2: 7; 1 Corinthians 15: 44), and therefore inseparable. In this unity, whatever befalls one befalls the other likewise. When God said to Adam "you are dust, and to dust you shall return" (Genesis 3: 19), God referred to the whole personality of man (body and soul) to undergo a complete death.

Since the doctrine of the immortality of souls contradicts with another doctrine of the resurrection of the body within the same creed, it seems important to stress on the doctrine of the resurrection of the body which affirms the creative work of God. God created the world and all that is in it. Since God is Creator, God is the one that will create a new life for people in the eschatological reality. To me, this understanding becomes a 'fact' that, of course, is open to disagreements.

Since there are as many interpretations as there are facts in various contexts, this book is important in various ways: first, it allows both scholars and novices realize the inapplicability of the clause in a current context different from the one in which the interpretations were done. Second, it allows scholars and normal interpreters to realize the importance of context, assumptions, and point of views in any interpretation being done. Third, it leaves an open question about the efficacy of the clause to people of the current context where it provides false promises to them about the possibility for mission in after death. Therefore, the book welcomes discussions from scholars and normal interpreters of the twenty first century with their own assumptions, contexts, and points of view.

Elia Shabani Mligo (PhD)
University of Iringa, Amani Centre
Njombe Tanzania
June, 2014

Acknowledgments

PART OF THIS BOOK is a re-worked version of Elikana Lova's Master Thesis for the Degree of Master of Christian Religion submitted to the Norwegian Lutheran School of Theology. It is not the same again, because we have added and removed many materials to bring it into a book form. However, we would like to give many sincere thanks to the following: first, both the Norwegian government and the Norwegian School of Theology for granting him a scholarship to study in their country. Second, his supervisor, Professor Jan Olav Henriksen, for his constructive and friendly supervision during the writing of the thesis.

Third, the group of people who made his stay in Oslo easy. It is possible to mention only a few of them: Mr. John T. Meyer, Dr. Tormond Engelsviken and Professor Karl Olav Sandness. Others are Rev. Arne J. Eriksen and the Fjellhaug Studentheim personnel.

Fourth, to Ms. Nancy Stevenson who corrected our English expressions to qualify for publication. The original version of the thesis did not have the corrections. Fifth, our colleagues both at Kidugala Lutheran Seminary and the University of Iringa – Amani Center at Njombe for sharing their ideas during our revision process.

Last, our family members: Lova's wife Judith and their son, young Erik-Asheri, for patiently staying alone in Tanzania for most of the time of Lova's studies in Oslo; and Mligo's wife Ester, for her encouragements during the many busy hours of revising the manuscript.

1

Introduction

SELECTING THE TOPIC

IT ALL BEGAN IN the Theological Education by Extension (TEE) class at Kidugala Lutheran Seminary[1] in 1993 when a certain Swedish missionary was teaching and trying to annul the belief in ancestors in African context. This was the time when we began feeling uncomfortable with the clause of Jesus' descent into hell of the Apostles' Creed. The Swedish missionary taught: "Once a person is dead, he is completely unable to communicate with the living. Therefore it is wastage of time and property to make sacrifices to the dead." With this affirmation we had no objection. What he spoke was a fact. Moreover, for us it was not only wastage of time and property to sacrifice to the dead, but also a foolish action. For the dead are dead in the real sense of the word. However, the missionary continued to explain his point: "When people die they go somewhere where they stay alive and are conscious, only that they

1. The Seminary is one of the institutions of the Evangelical Lutheran Church in Tanzania, Southern Diocese. It has a Bible School and Secondary school of both ordinary and high levels.

cannot communicate with the living. The story of Lazarus and the rich man (Luke 16:19–31) confirms the point."

Hearing this explanation we were startled. We could not expect to hear something of that sort from a person whom we thought was a learned theologian. We saw in him three kinds of theological problems: exegetical, dogmatic and practical. Exegetically, we found that his interpretation of the story of Lazarus and the rich man was too literal and wrong. From this story the missionary seemed to infer a local place where people go immediately after death. But, the fact is that, the story is a parable that presupposes the resurrection of the dead. It is a parable with an eschatological imprint requiring people to change their attitudes now in response to the preaching of their fellow common or ordinary human beings. The parable does not deny the possibility for persons to come from the dead (and to preach to the living) as the missionary was saying. It says, rather, that people may not believe even if the one preaching came from the dead. In this case the parable was anticipating the resurrection of Jesus himself. Hence, those people who did not believe in him before his death could not be convinced even by his resurrection.[2]

Dogmatically the missionary's argument was based on the doctrine of immortality of souls, which is not Christian but Greek. This in turn, according to our understanding, caused a practical problem for him; for it supported the very belief that he wanted to annul from his students. As Africans, if they still had the practice of making sacrifices to their ancestors, they would not have been hindered from continuing to do so by the teaching of this missionary. His teaching confirmed their belief that the dead were living. Had we not remembered the Apostles' Creed, we would have raised our hands and spoken our indignation about his teaching. But we remembered that here there is a mention that Christ descended into hell or to the dead. And what does that mean? We asked ourselves.

---

2. Cf. Black (ed.), *Peake's Commentary on the Bible,* 837; and Pfeiffer and Harrison (eds.), *The Wycliffe Bible Commentary,* 1055.

While formally we understood the descent as being another way of speaking about death and burial, now it suggested another meaning: The descent is Jesus' spatial transit to a local place of the death! With this meaning we deduced that, then, neither did Jesus really die, nor were those whom we thought to be dead really dead. Death has nothing serious to do with the termination of human life. For us this was a crisis of no mean order. Language seemed to have lost its meaning. Since that time we have never been happy with this question. Now we feel that this is the moment for us to do something about the descent into hell.

Many have written about this problem. However, none of them seems to have sensed its delicacy. All the possibilities for the doctrine of the descent cause some unwanted results, especially in teaching and preaching. For that reason we have decided to undertake this study so that we may point out that danger.

STATEMENT OF THE PROBLEM

In view of the above reason, the following is the statement of the problem: What is the real, non-ambiguous meaning and message of salvation that people receive from the teaching and preaching which refer to the doctrine of Christ's descent into hell? Is it true that the doctrine of Christ's descent into hell helps us in some way to understand the work of Christ as some theologians claim to be the case?[3] If it is true, what then does it imply concerning his being or nature; especially when hell is taken as an absolute eschatological punishment place or state for the wicked (cf. Matthew 5: 22, 29; Luke. 12: 5)? Can we still claim that Jesus was also divine if after his death was cast there?

Moreover, if hell is another name for *hades*, a local place for the souls of the dead, an interpretation which is popular to almost all world religions,[4] which also seems to be its meaning as it appears in the Creed, what can we say about Jesus' death and his

3. Stærk, "The Descent into Hell" (trans.), 104.

4. Cf. MacCulloch, *The Harrowing of Hell*, 1.

resurrection? Is it legitimate to speak of Jesus' vicarious death if his soul, which is the essence of human life and an inseparable entity of man, was not killed but continued to be alive in *hades*? How then could his "rising from the dead" be expressed as resurrection while in fact, as it would seem, it was just a simple re-uniting of his soul with the body? All these question need further scrutiny in the light of Christological study and the real practice of the current church in order to examine the implication of this doctrine to the teaching and practice of the current church.

MAJOR SOURCES USED IN THIS BOOK

The Bible is the first source for the development of this book. It contains a number of texts which are claimed to speak or allude to the doctrine of the descent. The main task in this book is to show how far those texts support or do not support the descent. However, it will be possible to comment on only a few of them.

The second source of material is the literature on Christian confessions. Here two works are chosen: Philip Schaff and Henry Wace (eds.). *A Select Library of Nicene and Post Nicene Fathers of the Christian Church*. Volume IV. Edinburgh: T. &T. Clark, 1987 and J. N. D. Kelly, *Early Christian Creeds*. London: Longman, 1972 (ed.). We have chosen these books because they both point out the time in the history of the production of the creeds when the descent first appeared. Kelly also provides some of the early interpretations of the descent.

The third source is J. A. MacCulloch, *The Harrowing of Hell: A Comparative Study of an Early Christian Doctrine*. Edinburgh: T. &T. Clark, 1930. This book is important to us because it is a classic defence of the doctrine of Jesus' descent into Hell. MacCulloch, all the way through his book, strives to prove that the descent is a sound Christian doctrine with no influence whatsoever from any of the many pagan myths which also have it.

The fourth group of literature is the classic works on Christology. These are Wolfhart Pannenberg, *What is Man? Contemporary Anthropology in Theological Perspective*. Philadelphia: Fortress

Press, 1970 and Jürgen Moltmann, *The Crucified God: The Cross of Christ as the Foundation and Criticism of Christian Theology.* London: SCM Press, 1974. We have chosen these classic books because they also discuss the question of Christ's descent into hell. Their approach is very dogmatical and different from that of the *Harrowing of Hell*. While MacCulloch understands Christ's descent into hell literally and takes the preaching to the dead and the harrowing of hell as being the purpose of the descent, for Pannenberg and Moltmann Jesus' descent into hell is understood figuratively. Together with other meanings, it basically signifies his passion. In fact, these sources were very helpful to us to discuss the Christological problem just highlighted above.

METHOD USED IN THIS BOOK

As we have just pointed out in the above line, the doctrine of the descent is a systematic theology issue, dealing with a dogmatical problem. It is our understanding that a person teaches and preaches what he/she believes to be true according to his/her dogmatical presuppositions.[5] The Christian faith is in the Triune God as it is expressed in its confessions grounded in the Bible. The nature of the confessions presupposes that those confessions become as free from ambiguities and unwanted implications as possible. This means that there has to be a thorough and systematic presentation of the doctrines or dogmas which are believed and which have to be transmitted through teaching or preaching for the belief and salvation of man. This thorough systematic presentation of doctrines has been the major task of systematic theology. Thus, if any fault is noted in a confession, the matter has to be dealt with systematically. This is mostly what is done in this book.

The other possible area in which the topic would fall is the New Testament. In this case the task to do some exegetical works on a number of texts would have been inevitable. But because of the limiting character of exegesis, and the fear of doing *eisegesis*,

5. Cf. 2 Corinthians 4: 13, ". . . 'I believed and so I spoke', we too believe, and so we speak."

we have decided to deal with the problem dogmatically, instead. This is also because the aim of the book is not very much that of interpretation of biblical texts; rather, it is to look at the interpretations of the descent as given by both New Testament commentators and dogmaticians; and hence, see if they are free from any misconceptions.

As the topic of this book indicates, the question to be discussed here is Christological. Therefore, in mentioning 'teaching' and 'preaching', it does not mean that there will be any pedagogical or homiletical works in the book. The words 'teaching' and 'preaching' are used here almost synonymously, to mean the proclamation of Good News or the transmission of the Christian faith. The aim is to show how the goal of this transmission may not be reached in some contexts due to the type of interpretations that are given to the descent doctrine.

AIM AND PROCEDURE

The aim of this book is to do a study on the meaning of the descent as it is stated in the Apostles' Creed, and its implications to Christian teaching and preaching within the current African church context. It is our thesis that the doctrine of the descent hardly fits the African context where ancestral cult is predominant. It is unfit because it encourages religious syncretism, and in doing that it makes teaching and preaching difficult in such context of the church.

In order to defend the above-stated thesis, the book is divided into three main parts: The first part is chapter two which presents some biblical references and historical information. It shows when and how the descent found its way into the Creed. The second part is the largest. It is comprised of chapters three, four, five, and six. This part deals with a number of meanings of the descent with reference to Christological implications. The third part deals with the practical problems of the descent. It shows how the descent has or might have already affected the message of the Church in African context. Last are a summary and some concluding remarks.

With the above aim and procedure, we hope that the materials presented and the argument of the book will be appealing to both scholars and students of systematic theology and other theological disciplines.

2

Apostolicity of the Descent

INTRODUCTION

THIS CHAPTER PROVIDES AN introductory material to the doctrine
of the descent. We present the concepts of Gehenna, *Hades* and
Sheol as discussed in both the Old and New Testaments, the two
types of death: physical and spiritual deaths, and the idea of immortality of souls. We also discuss MacClloch's examples of biblical references as his proofs for the doctrine of the descent. Hence,
in this chapter, we ascertain the way in which the doctrine of the
descent found its way in the Christian teaching and its apostolicity.

THE DESCENT DOCTRINE IN THE BIBLE

Jeremiah (7: 30–33) speaks of an offence committed by the sons of
Judah before God. They were sacrificing their children in Topheth,
which was in the valley of the sons of Hinnom. Having been an-
gered by that practice, God made the valley a burial place for the
bodies of people who died as a result of God's punishment. The
valley was to be an uncovered mass grave, where birds and beasts

could easily feast on the dead bodies. In Hebrew and its corresponding Aramaic word, the valley was called *Ge-Hinnom*.

According to later Jewish popular belief *Ge-Hinnom* came to be equated with hell or *gehena*, where the last judgement would take place.[1] Though Jeremiah 7: 32 suggests *gehena* was a burial place, besides being a place for punishment, the usual Old Testament word for the place of the dead is not *gehena*, but *sheol*. In *sheol* the dead are not only at rest, thoughtless and without knowledge or wisdom, but are also decomposing. Their bodies are full of maggots and words (cf. Ecclesiastes 9:10, Isaiah 14:11).

The New Testament word *gehena* corresponds to the *Ge-Hinnom* of Jeremiah 7:30–34. It is translated as hell. It appears mostly in the Gospels, and Jesus Christ himself speaks about it. For Jesus *gehena* is a place of fire reserved for punishing evil doers (Matthew 5: 22, 29–30; 10: 28; 23: 15, 33). The way Jesus speaks of punishment in hell, it presupposes that the judgement takes place after the general resurrection (cf. Matthew 25:31–46).[2] However, the usual New Testament word for the place of the dead is *hades* (Acts. 2: 27, 31, etc.). Its description is similar to that of *sheol* of the Old Testament. It has gates, and therefore it can be locked (Matthew 16: 8; Revelation 1: 18 Cf. Isaiah 38: 10). And then, just like *sheol*, *hades* often appears with the word "death" (or corruption or destruction) (Acts. 2:31; Revelation 1: 18; 20:13–15, cf. 2 Samuel 22: 6; Job 11: 8; Psalms 18: 5).

The way *hades* and death are used in the Bible sometimes convey the idea that they are used synonymously. Maybe that is why in some other places they raise some textual problems as to which of the two was intended to be written by the original author (Cf. Matthew 16: 18). The Bible talks of *sheol* and "destruction" that are never satisfied (Proverbs 27: 20, Isaiah. 5:14); and *hades* and death as riding on a horse waging war and killing a quarter of the world's inhabitants (Revelation 6: 8). This figurative description of the words can make one to ascribe something personal in

---

1. Kittel and Friedrich (eds.), *Theological Dictionary*, 113.

2. Also Cf. Kittel and Friedrich (eds.), *Theological Dictionary*, One Volume, 113.

them as if they were living beings. But they are not the only words in the Bible that are described in this way. For example, Psalms 118: 19 has: "open to me the gates of righteousness, that I may enter through them and give thanks to the LORD," just as death is said to come through the windows (Jeremiah 9: 21).

Hades/sheol is contrasted with heaven as presenting an opposite extreme. Thus Proverbs 15: 24 speaks of the wise man's path to lad upwards to life to avoid *sheol* beneath. In Isaiah 14: 12–15 the LORD speaks of the Day Star, the Son of Dawn, who boasts of ascending above the cloud to heaven, and above the stars of God, but he is brought down to *sheol*, to the depths of the pit. In the same manner Jesus warns Capernaum that she will not be exalted to heaven but will be brought down to *hades* (Matthew 11: 23 = Luke 10: 15). In this case, *hades/sheol* speaks of the reality of the fate of the wicked. It signifies the unpleasant place or situation that a person is supposed not to face. For it entails much distress and pain (cf. Luke16:23–24). It is the ultimate fate of the wicked (Proverbs 5: 5; 7: 27).

This understanding of *hades* corresponds to what the Bible speaks about death. Death signifies two realities. In the first place, death is a biological necessity for every - body. One is born unto death. Judges 13: 7 speaks of Samson being "a Nazirite to God from birth to the day of his death." Sickness causes death. Hezekiah was sick unto death (2 Kings 20:1, 2Chronicles 32: 24, etc., cf. John. 11: 4). However, though death can be taken to be the fate of every human being, the Bible does not stop there in speaking about it. It differentiates between the death of the sinner and the death of the righteous person. The death of the latter is a common death, but that of the former is not. The difference is in the manner of the deaths. The death of the righteous is preferred and prayed for (Numbers 23: 10), but that of the wicked is so disgraceful (cf. 1Kings. 22: 37–39).

This brings us to the second kind of death, namely spiritual death: the separation of humans from God (cf. Deuteronomy 29: 20–21). It is contrasted with eternal life: life in fellowship with God (John 1: 12; 3: 15). Figuratively, the death of the wicked brings a human down into *hades*, not heaven. The one who goes up to heaven is the one who dies the death of the righteous. The death of the righteous is said to be 'lifting' or 'taking up' as it is spoken of the death of Stephen (Acts. 8:1, 22: 20). The death of the wicked is therefore hell to him or her. It is hell in the sense that it separated him or her from the love and nearness of God.

However, the above discussion does not suggest a geographical location for hell or *hades* as the abode of souls of dead people. The belief of a local hell or *hades* is based on at least two points. First is the primitive view of the world as comprising of another world beneath the ground.[3] And second is the way one defines death to be the separation of soul from the body.[4] The latter leads or corresponds to the doctrine of the immortality of souls, which expresses one form of man's hope for life after death. It is contrasted with the idea of the resurrection of the body that presupposes a completely new mode of existence.[5]

Once it has been thought that a human being has a kernel in him, which can survive death, then the inevitable suggestion follows, that there must be a place where souls of humans go to wait for the last judgement. The common location has often been the underworld. Let us turn to this notion and examine it further in the next subsection.

JESUS' DESCENT INTO HELL IN BIBLICAL SCHOLARSHIP

The Biblical reference, which are discussed here, are those that are given by MacCulloch as his scriptural proofs of the descent. MacCulloch is choosen for this purpose because of his strong defence of the doctrine being apostolic, having no influence or resemblance from other religions of the world. Before he gives the Biblical references he first shows that the belief in a local hell is a global phenomenon. This is seen from the many examples of mythical

3. Cf. MacCulloch, *The Harrowing of Hell*, 4.

4. Cf. Vines, *Expository Dictionary of New Testament Words*. London: Oliphants, 1969 Sv. DEATH, DEATH-STROKE

5. Cf. Pannenberg, *What is Man?* 45.

stories he produces about the descent into the underworld. From the way he presents these examples of the universality of the belief, a certain pattern, however, is revealed which suggests that the belief in the descent may not have its origin in Christianity at all. He seems to portray something like an evolutionary theory of the development of the doctrine of the descent that finally finds its full expression in Christianity.

Basically the concern of all descent stories is for the communication between the living and the dead. In the first place these stories speak of dreams, hallucinations and trances as the medium through which one meets the spirits of the departed, either by the visit of the living to the dead or the dead himself coming to the living. Because of the affection relation between the living and the dead there involved another idea. A step from the possibility to fact took place: If men can go in dreams to *hades*, then they may also go while awake and rescue their lovers. Hence there are a vast number of tales concerning some mythical figures who went to rescue their relatives and other friends.[6]

The stories are very funny. The heroes who go there are said to be able to rescue their lovers only if the souls of the dead have not drunk of the well of the dead or eaten their foods. Stories about the rescuing of dead persons from *hades* are global. They are found, for example, in Polynesians and Ainu. They are also found in Africa, Eskimo land and China. Even Medieval Christianity knew of entrances to purgatory of hell. And until at the beginning of the 20th Century there was still a belief in Brittany of a hell that would be reached by a journey.

The more developed ideas on the doctrine of the descent describe *hades* as a place for both rest and punishment. For example, one Egyptian descent story depicts it to have various porches in which the righteous, wicked, and neutral souls are kept separately. MacCulloch identifies such stories as being parenetical. That is, they teach a dogmatical eschatology, warning people against unrighteous living.[7] Stories about the descent, therefore, seem to

6. MacCulloch, *The Harrowing of Hell*, 3.

7. *Ibid.*, 9.

have been told at two levels of motives. In the lower stage of their development they were concerned with the rescuing of the dead by their living lovers. But in the higher forms of religions the descent is for the purpose of enlightening the dead or freeing them from torment and for dogmatical instruction.[8]

In connection with the two levels above, there is another level that is more abstract than the first two. Here are stories that are connected with the belief that the living person can remit pain from a tormented dead person and transfer him to a state of bliss. Thus in Buddhism, the tormented can warmly be refreshed by rays thronging into hell from a smiling Buddha. And in other religions prayers and sacrifices are the means by which the tormented are helped.

This kind of belief is found not only in the so-called higher religions, e.g. Judaism, and in the theological conception of purgatory in Christianity, but also in the religions of the so called 'savages.' Thus the Talmud exhorts the living to give offerings and prayers in order to shorten the stay of the dead in *gehena*. And while an African from Lesotho is busy sacrificing his bull and praying at the grave of this relative in order to secure him a happy reception in the underworld, for a similar purpose, the Christian is indulging in indulgences.[9]

In view of the above discussion one wonders whether the descent is a Christian doctrine or a borrowed thing, or just a popular belief held by both Christians and non-Christians alike. MacCulloch would not like any of the ideas above. For him, the Apostles taught about the descent, and therefore it is a sound scriptural doctrine. In order to support his affirmation he takes Paul, John, and Peter as his main reference points. Here are only a few examples of texts MacCulloch thinks are important for the descent doctrine. The first text that claims to refer to the descent is Ephesians 4: 8: "when he ascended on high he led a host of captives, and gave gifts to men." Paul quotes this verse from Psalms 68: 18: "Thou didst ascend the high mount, leading captives in thy train, and receiving

---

8. *Ibid.,* 10.

9. MacCulloch, *The Harrowing of Hell*, 33.

gifts among men, even among the rebellious, that the LORD God may dwell there."

MacCulloch interprets the 'captives' to mean the 'spirits in prison' of 1 Peter 3: 19. He mentions the Church Fathers, e.g., Origen, as also having the same interpretation. And then he comes up with a conclusion that this verse from Ephesians 4: 8, especially when taken together with 4: 9, is a direct reference to Christ's descent and rescue of souls kept in *hades*. He substantiates his conclusion with other texts, like Colossians 2: 15, Philippians 2: 10 and 1 Corinthians 15: 55, which speak of the submission of every creation to Christ. However, one wonders whether this is a fair interpretation of the text concerned.

The smallest context of this text is verses 7–13, which deal with a description of the diversity of gifts. Here Paul is speaking about one practical side of the Church, which is unity. For him unity is achieved in the diversity of gifts that are bestowed to the Church by the ascended Christ. When Paul mentions the descent, his purpose is to emphasise the importance of humility, which is opposed to pride, that leads to Christian disunity. His thesis is that Christ was exalted so as to become the dispenser of gifts just because he had first humiliated himself. The genitive in the phrase, "the lower parts of the earth," is not a genitive of location, which could mean the interior of the earth's crust or *hades*. Rather, it is a genitive of opposition referring to the incarnation and Christ's coming to earth (Cf. John 3: 13).

Furthermore, the mention of knees in heaven, on earth and underground in Philippians 2: 10 should not be forced to support elaborate theories of classification of the universe and thus affirm the existence of a local *hades*.[10] Rather, this is only an expression of a universality and the totality of created rational beings who will pay due homage to Christ. More likely, MacCulloch understands wrongly the expression that Christ 'leads captivity captive'. He identifies those who were led with the rescued souls formerly kept in captivity or *hades*. The meaning here, however, is that Christ overpowered that which had overpowered human beings

10. Pfeiffer and Harrison (eds.), *The Wycliffe Bible Commentary*, 1325.

and annulled its power. Therefore the captives who are referred here are not the beneficiaries of the work of Christ, but they are adversaries who are taken captives by him.

This is the very meaning of Psalms 68: 18, which also explains what happened on the cross according to 1Corinthians 2: 15. For Paul the crucifixion is the decisive contest in which the hostile powers that held mankind in their grip were openly defeated and made captive, of which death is one of them (1 Corinthians 15: 55).[11] Therefore the claim that Paul referred to Christ having gone to rescue souls of men in *hades* is possibly not a legitimate one.

The second text, which MacCulloch claims to refer to Christ's descent into hell, is Revelation 1: 18. For him this text is an affirmation that John knew about the descent. It is not only MacCulloch who thinks so. Also for others, like Turner, this verse implies that "through death Christ visits Hades and preaches."[12] However, this interpretation is not a right one. This is not the right one because it does not take into account the context and genre in which the text is situated.

The reference to the keys of personified death and *hades* simply means that the destiny of humanity is entirely under the jurisdiction of Christ. This is clearly seen elsewhere in John's writings. In John 11: 25–26, for example, it is reported, "Jesus said to her, 'I am the resurrection and the life, he who believes in me, though he dies, ye shall he live, and whoever lives in me shall never die. Do you believe this?'" Jesus spoke these words before his death and resurrection. Thus, his power over death does not necessarily depend on the fact that he died and was resurrected. He had power over it even before that. The episode of the rising of Lazarus also confirms this point. Jesus did not need to die himself in order to set the soul of Lazarus free after unlocking the 'gates' of *hades* with 'keys'. For him it was enough to stand at the door of the tomb and call the dead out. Therefore Revelation 1: 18 should not be taken in

11. Cf. Black (ed.), *Peake's Commentary,* 993. See also Pfeiffer &.Harrison (eds.), *The Wycliffe Bible Commentary,* 1310, 1341 and Reinecker, *A Linguistic Key,* 531.

12. Black (ed.), *Peake's Commentary,* 1048.

isolation. Without forgetting that the text pertains to apocalyptic literature, whose affinity for figurative language is great, the text has to be interpreted in the light of the whole Johannine concept of life.

The last texts to be discussed are 1 Peter 3: 19 and 4: 6. The texts are important because it seems that many people who speculate about life after death and the descent of Jesus into hell use them. Staerk, for example, notes that in Norway there is a strong tradition which links the descent with 1 Peter 3: 19.[13] Also, for Lenski, who takes the whole pericope of 3:18—4:6 as being just simple, explains that when Christ's body lay dead in the tomb, his soul was in heaven; and that when the time for the descent came, his soul suddenly reunited with his body and in that instant Christ in his human body went to the dead as Peter reports.[14] Lenski boldly discusses this question of how and when Christ descended into hell as if he were present and witnessed the whole drama!

However, others admit ignorance and do not pretend to know too much about this text. Luther, for example, is reported to have once written, "A wonderful text is this and a more obscure passage perhaps than any other in the New Testament, so that I do not know for certainty just what Peter means."[15] Here Luther points to one important fact, that the text has no straightforward interpretation. This point is also noted by Clowney, who says that the text was without doubt understood by the people to whom Peter was writing, but not by the people of today.[16]

The obscurity of the text, according to our point of view, is also shown by the fact that even those who understand it as speaking about Jesus' descent into *hades* differ very much in asserting the form in which Jesus went there and about the recipients of his preaching. While some speak of the soul as being the subject of the descent, others say it was the vivified or resurrected body.

13. Staerk, "The Descent into Hell." (trans.), 6.

14. Lenski, *The interpretation of I and II Epistles of Peter,* 161.

15. Clowney, *The Message of 1Peter,* 156.

16. *Ibid.*

Concerning the addresses of the message, others say that they were the disobedient spirits or angels or demons. And others speak of the patriarchs of Israel. Further, there is no agreement even concerning the content of the message itself: whether it was a pronouncement of doom or salvation depends on how one is able to convince the mass. It is not the interest of the authors of this book to go into that discussion. After all much has already been written about it, e.g., by Clowney.[17] What is important here is to decide whether 1 Peter 3: 19 and 4: 6 refer to Christ's descent into hell.

It is interesting to note that MacCulloch, who insists that the Fathers taught the descent, is not able to hide the fact that Augustine and Aquinas did not agree that the texts were speaking of Christ having gone to *hades*. For them the 'quickening in spirit' meant 'quickened by the Holy Spirit'. They objected to the notion that the soul of Christ went to preach to the dead. Also for them, 'spirits in prison' did not refer to souls of men in *hades*, but in the "darkness of ignorance while yet still in bodies of men."[18]

MacCulloch who does not agree with this interpretation is in favour of the Syriac version which reads '*sheol*' or '*hades*' for 'prison', which, according to Revelation 20: 7; 2Baruch 23: 4 and 2 Esdras 7: 95, refer to the lower part of the underworld, the prison of Satan, where souls are guarded. One thing about MacCulloch's use of Scriptures is that he seems to count Apocryphal writings as also being important Christian writing that can be referred to without any reservation. Thus, others, who look at those writings with indifference, may not be able to assign much value to his arguments.

Second, there are some Biblical references that even a simple reader of the Bible may not fail to see that they are violently forced to speak on the descent. For example, Isaiah 42: 7; 49: 1 and 61: 1, MacCulloch takes them to be Isaiah's prophesy about the release of souls from *hades*![19] MacCulloch is well aware that not all readers

17. Clowney, *The Message of 1 Peter*, 154.

18. MacCulloch, *The Harrowing of Hell*, 51.

19. MacCulloch, *The Harrowing of Hell*, 51.

accept 1 Peter as pointing to Jesus' visit to *hades*. Despite all this he stands firm in his idea. He says, "Whether the Petrine passages refer to the descent or not, the doctrine itself, wherever derived, soon became a most vital one in early Christian thought."[20]

Swete reveals how the descent doctrine finds support from the Scriptures. For him, the early legends of the descent ere not based on Peter's words. But, "their general acceptance may with more probability be traced to the influence of some early teaching which strove to combine the scattered hints of scriptures."[21] From Swete's arguments and from the way MacCulloch uses the Bible, one evidently sees that the descent is not derived form the Bible, but the Bible is being used to confirm the belief which is already held in the minds of the people.

Coming to the close of this section, it can be concluded that it is doubtful whether the descent doctrine is Biblical. For even 1 Peter 3:19, which for MacCulloch is an important text for the doctrine, for others it has only a secondary effect. For example, Bo Reiche, who has written a monograph dealing particularly with this verse, notes that the verse has played no essential part in the history of the descent.[22] And for Schwarz, the descent doctrine cannot be derived from Peter or from any passage in the whole NT, for "the descent into the realm of the dead is nowhere explicitly stated in the New Testament."[23]

IMMORTALITY OF SOULS AND THE RESURRECTION

The claim of MacCulloch that the descent doctrine is derived form the Bible is disproved in the preceding discussion. No apostle or any of the NT writers can be claimed to have had explicitly expressed the belief about Christ's descent into hell. Though it cannot

20. *Ibid.* 65.

21. *Ibid.*

22. Reicke, *The Disobedient Spirits*, 10.

23. Schwarz, *Responsible Faith*, 254.

be denied that the doctrine once became a vital one in the history of Christianity, it is evident that it is derived from the universal concept of the immortality of the soul. For its basic presupposition is that the soul of a person continues to survive after his death. The concept of immortality of souls is one of the answers to man's quest for the hope of life beyond death. It is derived from the conception that man is constituted of body and soul, the former being mortal and the latter immortal.

Pannenberg, who contrasts the two kinds of hope of life beyond death, the immortality of souls and the resurrection of the dead, explains how the former was developed in Greek philosophy. He says that for the earlier Greeks the soul only meant the animating spirit which is exhaled out by a dying man. They did not attribute any immortality to it. However, later on Plato gave it a further qualification. For him the soul was the perceptive entity of man which had a participation in the eternal archetypes from which the physical things are recalled. This participation of man's soul in the eternal archetypes presupposes that this soul knew them before it was chained in the body. And that since archetypes are imperishable, then, so is the soul.

Pannenberg recounts that though Plato's theory of man's soul's participation in these original ideas of things has never found support among many scholars, his concept of the soul as being a separate and different entity from man's body has "stubbornly persisted."[24] Pannenberg seems to be right in characterising the concept of the immortality of the soul as stubborn. Its stubbornness can be seen, for example, in Vine's definition of death. He defines it as "the separation of the soul (the spiritual part of man) from the body (the material part), the latter ceasing to function and turning to dust."[25] And he claims that this is the way death is defined in the Bible. The texts he gives to substantiate his definition are John 11: 13, Hebrews 2: 15; 5: 7 and 7: 23. However, one wonders that not only is the idea of the separation of the soul from

---

24. Pannenberg, *What Is Man?* 47.

25. Vine, *Expository Dictionary* (1969).

the body not contained in those texts but also, in fact, these texts are not concerned at all with giving a definition of death!

Anyway, according to Pannenberg, modern anthropology does not see man as being constituted of two separate entities: one corporeal and another non-corporeal. It sees him as a unified corporeal creature, just as all animals are. For modern anthropology, if there is any difference between man and animals, then that difference is not explained in terms of a kernel in man that can survive death, but in behavioural difference. That is, man has one kind of behaviour and an animal has another kind. Pannenberg explains this difference in behaviour, as being constituted in the fact that while man is 'open to the world' the animal is not. That is, man does not depend only on his instinct for his survival, nor does he live in the total present, as the animal does.

From this fact Pannenberg derives the two concepts immortality of souls and resurrection, showing how they came to be expressions of man's hope for life beyond death. He explains that though man is able to manipulate many situations and create an artificial environment suitable for his life, he always faces many limitations and frustrations. Faced with these limitations and lack of satisfaction in his/her present life, human's behavior of openness to the world makes him/her project his/her satisfaction in the future, and beyond the world, that is beyond death. At this stage then comes the juncture of how this hope finds expression. The Greeks offer the concept of the immortality of the soul as man's hope and yearning for life after death. In this case, nothing significantly changes between the person who lives now and the one who continues to live after death.

Christianity offers the second kind of hope for life after death in the concept of the resurrection of the body. In this case nothing in man survives death. And the resurrected being is really a new creation.

The concept of resurrection of the body takes death seriously as the end of everything that pertains to present life, although even in death man is still in God's hand. According to Pannenberg the concept of immortality of souls cannot be an adequate explanation even of the fact that man is always, whether dead or alive, in God's presence. For in the concept of the immortality of souls the "seriousness of death, which means an end to everything that we are, is misunderstood."[26]

While MacCulloch insists that the concept of the descent, which as it has been seen, presupposes the immortality of soul, to have no influence from outside Christianity, others would say that even the Christian concept of the resurrection of the dead, which expresses appropriately the hope for life beyond death, has its origin not in Christianity itself. According to Pannenberg the Persians and not the Jews first held the expectation of a future resurrection of the dead. The Jews took it from the Persians, and Christians and Muslims adopted it as well. However, Pannenberg does not mean to demean or desacralize the concept of resurrection because he admits Persian influence. But he would say that it was adopted in the Jewish-Christian society because it "converged with the requirements of the history of traditions in Israel."[27]

To conclude this section, we can now say that the doctrine of Christ's descent into hell is not apostolic. This is because the doctrine presupposes the idea of the immortality of souls, which, not only is Greek, but also not explicitly expressed in the New Testament.

THE DESCENT IN THE SIRMIUM CREED

The situation in which the clause of the descent into hell first appeared in the creed was not a blessing to the Church, but mourning. The whole Church had succumbed to Arianism in which bishops were forced to subscribe to the Arian confession of faith. By the edict of the emperor everybody had to sign this confession or else face the consequence. Jerome describes the situation as one in which "the whole world groaned and wondered to find itself Arian."[28]

26. Pannenberg, *What Is Man?* 49.

27. *Ibid.*, 52.

28. Kelly, *Early Christian Creeds*, 292.

After the council of Nicaea (A.D. 325), a number of bishops who belonged to the Arian party, with Eusebius as their leader, were not content with the proceedings and the formula of the Nicene Council. Together with having a strategy of deposing bishops from their sees, those who had been the main speakers of the Nicene, Athanasius being one of them, began holding meetings, one after the other. In each, they came up with their own confession of faith that, in content, opposed that of the Nicene.[29]

During a short period, from A.D. 335–357, they had produced seven confessions, most of them in the presence of the Emperor Constantius, the son of Constantine. The severity of their attack on the Nicene formula increased as they continued to produce more creeds. However, in all these confessions, all Eastern, there was no clause about the descent of Jesus into hell.

The clause of Jesus' descent into hell came into the creedal formula with the triumph of Arianism when Constantius became the sole emperor of both East and West from A.D. 353 to 361. In A.D. 359 Constantius attended a council at Sirmium and in his favour the so-called 'dated' creed was published. According to Athanasius, this was the eighth Arian confession[30] which, with the reinforcement of the emperor, immediately circulated to all churches. Mainly Western bishops, as Kelly notes, attended the Sirmium council.[31] The Sirmium creed is called the 'dated' creed because it mentions the date of its publication. It was May 22, 359. Athanasius, together with other reasons, criticises it because of its mention of the date. He wondered whether their faith had only begun on that date and was not apostolic.

It is not the scope of this book to give a presentation on the doctrinal controversy of which the Arians were disputing with the advocates of the Nicene Creed. Suffice it to say that it was the question of whether the Son was of the same essence, *homoousios*,

---

29. Schaff and Wace (eds.), *A Select Library of Nicene and Post-Nicene Fathers*, 97.

30. Schaff and Wace (eds.) *A Select Library of Nicene and Post-Nicene Fathers*, 454.

31. Kelly, *Early Christian Creeds*, 285.

with the Father or not. For the Nicene party he was and for the Arians he was not. The latter detested the idea that the Son, too, was eternal and divine.

It is in this creed, the Sirmium or dated Creed, where Christ's descent into hell is first mentioned in a creedal formula. It is not understood why the descent clause was added at this time. For the only problem of the time, as it has just been pointed out, was whether divinity could be ascribed also to Christ or not. From the Sirmium Creed it would seem that the descent found its way in one Aquileian Creed, which was one of the many variants, about fourteen, of the so-called Old Roman baptismal creed. And from here it was incorporated into the Apostles' Creed, which is a modification of one of the variants of the Old Roman creed.[32]

From the fact that the three creeds, the Dated, Aquileian, and the Apostles', are Western, it may not be wrong to infer that the descent clause is a Western invention. However, when it comes to the real origin of the doctrine, Kelly mentions the East. He appeals to the historian Socrates whom he quotes as having pointed to Mark of Arethusa, a Syrian, to be the author of the descent. Then, he substantiates Socrates' theory by giving his own examples that show that the descent figured very early in Eastern creed material. One example he gives is the Syrian *Didascalia* which, he says, echoes creedal language when it asks, "who was crucified under Pontius Pilate and departed in peace, in order to preach to Abraham, Isaac and Jacob and all the saints concerning the ending of the world and the resurrection of the dead."[33]

He further points to other references in the works of one Apharates and in the Acts of Thomas of the third century. Then he concludes, "Thus, although it never caught on in official Eastern creed . . . it is very likely that the West admitted it to its formularies under Eastern influences."[34] A question then, which could be asked here, is about the motive for the insertion of the descent clause into the creed. One thing, however, which can be mentioned here,

32. Cf. Kelly, *Early Christian Creeds*, 378.
33. Ibid., 379.
34. Kelly, *Early Christian Creeds*, 379.

is that, though the clause first appeared in a polemical creed, the clause itself had dogmatic significance other than polemical.[35]

Kelly mentions at least two reasons for its being accepted in the West. First, he says that it was an expression of the wishful imaginations of Christians to dwell in the Saviour's experiences in the underworld. And this is seen from the many and often fantastic attempts to portray them in art. Secondly, Kelly mentions that by the time the descent were incorporated into the creed, the ancient notion that Christ had a mission to the Old Testament patriarchs was fading away. And therefore the clause had a supplementary function in providing "the creed with something which had hitherto been lacking and of which the need may have been keenly, if inarticulately, felt, a mention of the act of redemption wrought by Christ."[36] That is, the clause was interpreted as symbolising Christ's triumph over Satan and death, and hence, the salvation of all mankind. The discussion of these meanings of the descent, and others, will be carried out soon in the following chapters.

CONCLUSION

The major concern of this chapter was to survey the origin and apostolicity of the descent doctrine. It has been vivid from this chapter that the doctrine can hardly be claimed to be biblical because none of the apostles proclaimed it. The doctrine is thought to originate from popular beliefs of immortality of souls that were embraced by various religious beliefs of the early Christian era. Moreover, it has been found out that the motive for the insertion of the descent clause in the Apostles' Creed was people's hope for life beyond death as derived from the idea of immortality of souls which is not only Greek, but universal. However, as it will be seen later, this is deferent from the hope that is expressed in the Christian doctrine of resurrection of the body. Thus, this means that the doctrine of the descent had no Christian origin.

---

35. Ibid., 382. Also cf. Staerk, "The Descent into Hell" (trans.), 18.
36. *Kelly, Early Christian Creeds*, 383.

3

Jesus Christ the Saviour

INTRODUCTION

IN THE PREVIOUS CHAPTER we discussed about the origin and apostolicity of the descent doctrine. In this chapter we will deal with the content of the doctrine of the descent and its implication to our current understanding. The purpose is to present the diverse meanings of the descent and measure their conformity to the basic Christian teaching about Christ and his work. Some of the questions raised in this chapter are the following: What is the relationship between the doctrine of the descent and Jesus' work on earth? What is the relationship between Jesus' death and the asserted victory in hell? Is it plausible to shift the victory of Jesus from the cross to the preaching in hell? Is it possible to do mission to our dead relatives who died in sin? In trying to respond to these and other related questions, the chapter explores Luther's "happy exchange" theology of the cross in relation to the doctrine of the descent. It also explores the relationship between the doctrine of the descent and the humanity of Jesus.

CHRIST'S DESCENT
AS THE FINALIZATION OF HIS WORK

The first interpretation of the descent claims that Christ had a similar duty in hell just like the one he had on earth before his death. The functional intention of Christ's descent into the underworld is hinted from the very beginning when the idea of the descent is introduced into the creedal formula of Sirmium. There it is stated that Christ had "died, and descended to the underworld and regulated things there, whom the gate keepers of hell saw and shuddered."[1] No further explanation is given to the kind of tasks, which Christ did in hell. However, a double task of preaching to the dead and the harrowing of hell is the one, which seems to be in the minds of many.[2] That Christ went to hell and did something there was also the belief of the Reformers or theologians of the Augsburg Confession. However, for them it was not the soul of Christ that was the subject of the descent, but the entire person of Christ, as God and man.

Despite this belief among the Reformers, the doctrine of Jesus' descent into hell was not a simple one for them. Because of this fact they made a resolution to stop further disputations and speculations concerning the article. For them it was enough to know that Christ went there and "conquered the devil, destroyed hell's power and took from the devil his might."[3] Simplicity of faith was required. Though the Reformers did not mention any problem entailed in the speculations about the descent, today it is found that the doctrine raises too many problems that are difficult to solve.

At present we are going to deal with one question that claims that Christ's descent is an extension of his work. The idea contained in this question is that if Christ had to fully complete his work of salvation then he also had to go and preach to the dead and confront Satan right at his barracks. The advocates

1. Kelly, *Early Christian Creeds*. 378.
2. MacCulloch, *The Harrowing of Hell*, 217.
3. Tappert (ed.), *The Book of Concord*, 610.

of this claim see in it a final triumph of Jesus over Satan and a universal salvific work of Jesus even to those who did not live during Jesus' activity on earth.[4] They do not see the earthly work of Christ and his cross to have been enough if he had not gone to the underworld too. In other words, it is as if they want to say that it was necessary that Jesus died, for in so doing he had the chance to visit hell. His death is thus taken to be like a door through which he was able to enter hell.

The notion that Christ had to die so that he could get the chance to visit hell drives us to equate his death with the deaths of the many martyrs who died with the same kind of hope or intention in their minds. For example, as Moltmann notes, Socrates died as a wise man whose death was "testimony to the immortality of souls . . . (and) a break through to a higher, pure life."[5] Moltmann also mentions the Zealots who were crucified by the Romans. They willingly accepted their deaths because of their conviction of dying as righteous men before God. They hoped ultimately to triumph over their adversaries. The same, he says, is true of Christian martyrs. They calmly approached death because they were conscious of being crucified with Christ. And, as for Dietrich Bonhoeffer, his death was not something very fearful with a dark end. Before his execution he is reported to have said, "This is the end for me the beginning of life."[6] Thus, it would seem that his death, for him, like all martyrs, was not catastrophic, but tolerable.

However, when it comes to Jesus' death, the matter is very different. In the words of Moltmann, Jesus' death was not a 'fine death'. He was greatly distressed and troubled (Mark 15: 37, Hebrews 5: 7).[7] According to Molmann, Jesus' death cannot be compared with the deaths of martyrs simply because he did not die hoping in anything. He died in despair. For his death meant not

---

4. Cf. Pannenberg. *What Is Man?* 272; MacCulloch, *The Harrowing of Hell*, 325; Reicke, *The Disobedient Spirits*, 33; and Stærk, "The Descent into Hell" (trans.), 80 and 90.

5. Moltmann, *The Crucified God*, 145.

6. *Ibid.*, 146.

7. *Ibid.*

only the end of his life, but also his cause for which he lived and worked. In this death Jesus found himself to be forsaken by his Father and God whose closeness and grace he himself had proclaimed. Therefore to state that Christ's descent into hell was for the finalization of his work is to say that he died with some kind of hope. But as it is observed, he did not have any, except misery.

CHRIST'S DESCENT
AND THE THEOLOGY OF THE CROSS

People like Althaus and Luther, when speaking about the death of Christ, have preferred to talk and emphasise the significance of the cross to the extent that they have become known as the theologians of the cross.[8] But now, with the doctrine of the descent it would seem that the emphasis is moving to hell where, together with defeating the devil, Christ preached to the dead. That is, here, another significance of Jesus' death is suggested: Its significance lies not only in the fact that through it the living is saved, but in the fact that through it, it was possible for him to visit hell.

It is this significance that makes people like Stærk to feel sorry that many people are not aware of the value of Jesus' descent. And therefore, for Stærk, it becomes one of his reasons to write a thesis so that he calls the attention of even the average Christian to become conscious of it.[9] The shift to hell seems to locate the final victory of Jesus over the powers that had kept men captive not on the cross, but in *hades* or hell. Here we see that the meaning of the cross is obscured. In this case Luther's 'happy exchange' theory, which is one of the substances of the theology of the cross, with its emphasis in Jesus' suffering; that through it we are purchased, killed and made alive,[10] is found to be meaningless. The problem there is that we are forced to assign this happy exchange also to the souls of dead men in *hades*, not only to the living on earth.

8. Cf. Braaten and Jenson (eds.), *Christian Dogmatics,* 49.

9. Stærk, "The Descent into Hell" (trans.), 1.

10. Braaten and Jenson (eds.) *Christian Dogmatics,* 50.

However, in doing so, first we will not be able to tell what was the nature of the exchange between Jesus and the souls of the dead in *hades*, unless we indulge ourselves in speculations. Second, as it is already been said earlier, the suggested necessity to do mission also to the dead relatives obstructs the idea of the vicarious nature of Jesus' death, which is the presupposition of the theology of the cross.

The theory of happy exchange is, however, based upon the fact that God succeeded in giving oneself to us sinners, who are living here on earth, bore our sin and destroyed the barriers between us and himself through Christ's actual coming to us, his cross and resurrection, by giving his sinless and righteous nature. Only in this manner is Luther able to mention the efficacy of the Lord's Supper, that in and by it, by the blood of Christ, the wrath of God is placated as human sins are forgiven. That is, when the body and blood given to us are received in faith, God's wrath is placated.[11]

Now, it is not possible to give such an interpretation to Jesus' death if the descent is made the reason for his death. Only when the cross is taken seriously can we be able to assign the 'happy exchange' in Jesus' death.

CHRIST'S DESCENT
AS AN AFFIRMATION OF HIS HUMANITY

Some people claim that the doctrine of Christ's descent into hell has contributed to the understanding of the work of Christ. This claim can be seen, for example in Stærk's praises of the doctrine when he says, "There is every reason to be happy about the content in the doctrine of the descent of Christ into *hades*: Now we know that he has completed the work."[12] For Stærk, however, the completion of Christ's work does not comprise in the harrowing of hell or any other activity in hell, because the devil was already beaten on the cross. For him Christ's descent affirms and reminds

11. *Ibid.*

12. Stærk, "The Descent into Hell" (trans.), 104.

people that Christ was really a human being who had to follow a rule that is valid for all men who die. That is, the fact that Christ's soul had a stay among the souls of other dead men in *hades*, affirms that Jesus, as a true man, really died and was buried. As such, the insertion of the descent clause in the creed is taken to have had the intention of adding weight to this fact of the death and humanity of Jesus.

The claim in this interpretation of the descent to affirm Christ's humanity gives the idea that people had some doubts about it. However, the Gospels' narratives give a quite reverse understanding of people about him. They never thought that he was not a human being. Take, for example, the Gospel according to Mark, throughout it his contemporaries regarded Jesus as only man. It was very difficult for them to see him as divine, though from time to time they were reminded by demons of that fact. In all encounters with demons, they identified Jesus as the Son of God.

Human beings, not even those who were direct beneficiaries of his healing, gave no title that identified him as divine. For them he was just a man from Nazareth or the Son of David, a human being just like themselves. Even the accusation of blasphemy, with which Jesus was accused, was based on the people's firm conviction that he was a mere man who pretended to be God. Nor can the community in which the belief of Christ's descent into hell first appeared to be claimed to have had doubts about his true humanity. Kelly, who traces its first inception to a Syrian speaking locality, points out that initially the descent was regarded "as no more that a more colourful equivalent of DEAD and BURIED."[13]

Even when the descent travelled westwards and was inserted in the Apostles' Creed, the motive for its admission was not polemical. It only "symbolised His triumph over Satan and death, and, consequently, the salvation of mankind as a whole."[14] Therefore, the motive to affirm Christ's humanity is only being forced here.

13. Kelly, *Early Christian Creeds*, 383.
14. *Ibid.*

The other idea, which is conveyed in the argument that the descent into hell affirms Christ's humanity, is that the descent put weight or validated his work. In this case hell overtakes the significance of his resurrection. However, people like Elert and Althaus would not ascribe such significance to hell. For them the only event that validates Jesus' work is his resurrection. This assertion is based on the fact that Jesus' death had called into question his pre-Easter work. People were shaken in their belief about him because of his death. But it was the resurrection that became the basis of their faith in him. It was from Easter that faith in Christ began to be lived.[15]

Elert and Althaus are discussing the question of whether the mere person of the earthly Jesus was the ground of faith for the first believers. They disagree with people like Hermann who think that the mere person of Christ was enough to create faith apart from his resurrection. Though in their context these two theologians are not dealing with the question of Christ's descent into hell, nothing could have hindered them mentioning it if it had any significance.

CONCLUSION

The content of the doctrine of the descent is mostly intriguing in the way it is presented in relation to the work of Jesus. As it has been noted, the doctrine of the decent seems to assert that Jesus' work could be incomplete without the visitation and preaching in hell. It emphasizes that the preaching of Jesus in hell was necessary in order to make his work utterly complete and firm. In suggesting this necessity the doctrine also suggests for the need to do mission to the dead relatives in hell.

The main obscuring issue in relation to the doctrine of the descent is the shift in emphasis. If we accept that hell was the consummation of Jesus work, then the main emphasis is hell as a place of Jesus victory over death which goes contrary to Luther's happy exchange theology of the cross whose emphasis is the cross as a

---

15. Pannenberg, *Jesus-God and Man*, 108.

place of Jesus' victory; and in that way obscuring the whole teaching of the church.

We can briefly conclude that Christ's descent cannot be claimed to affirm his humanity simply because at the time when it was inserted in the creed no one doubted about his humanity and it was not inserted for polemical purpose. Nor can it be a validation of his work, only because the resurrection does that.

4

The States of Christ
and His Descent into Hell

INTRODUCTION

THE PREVIOUS CHAPTER DISCUSSED about the validity of some
interpretations of Jesus' descent into hell in relation to his work as
Saviour. We argued that Jesus' decent into hell cannot be claimed
to be the finalization of his work. We concluded that the emphasis
on Jesus' victory cannot be located in hell but on the cross. We
further showed that The very assertion that Jesus' work could be
incomplete without his preaching in hell was not only opposed to
Luther's theology of the cross, but also adds more problems to the
earthly mission of the church because it suggests for the possibility
of doing mission to the dead relatives contrary to the Christian
teaching about human salvation.

This chapter examines two interpretations of the descent
doctrine in relation to the two states of Christ, namely the exaltation and humiliation. It is our observation that the descent into
hell cannot be humiliation because the maximum humiliation
of Jesus, according to Christian teaching, took place at the cross.

Moreover, Jesus descent into hell cannot be his exaltation because his exaltation took place at his resurrection.

CHRIST'S DESCENT AS HIS HUMILIATION

As stated in the introduction above, there are two interpretations of the descent that are linked with the so-called states of Christ (which are humiliation and exultation). The question that has been discussed in history has been to which state the descent should be assigned. The Reformed theologians of the sixteenth century interpreted Christ's descent into hell as the lowest point of his state of humiliation and many theologians have followed this interpretation today.

Braaten who also follows this line of interpretation describes the humiliation in this way, "The downward curve of the incarnational line reaches its lowest point in Jesus' descent into hell."[1] He gives two significant points about the descent depending on whether *hades* (a place for the dead) or hell (a place for the damned) is referred to. In the case of the latter, Christ's descent signifies the extent of his suffering and humiliation for the sake of humankind. And if *hades* is the one referred to, then Christ's descent signifies the universality of his work of salvation that reaches "beyond the limits of those who preach and hear the gospel in this life."[2]

In this section we are going to deal with the line of discussion that takes hell as the place of the damned and claims that Jesus also went there. The argument here revolves around the fact that Jesus bore the sins of the world. And as the sinner is destined for fire in hell, then, Jesus, too, had to suffer it. Stærk mentions Hagin Kenyon as describing this kind of Jesus' suffering as a "Satisfactory Suffering."[3]

Having presented this line of thought, we will then evaluate it, whether it contributes positively to the understanding of Christ and his work. The argument that Christ paid the penalty for human sin

1. Braaten and Jenson (eds.), *Christian Dogmatics,* 548.
2. Ibid., 549.
3. Stærk, "The Descent into Hell" (trans.), 35.

is valid, but it is not right to locate this penalty in hell. According to the Bible and especially what Jesus himself spoke of hell, hell is an eschatological reality which will be experienced by evil doers (cf. Matthew 25: 31–46). It is an absolute, non-reversible reality. Once one is brought to that place there is no chance of escaping, just like the rich man (Luke16: 19–31) was not able even to reduce the degree of the pain inflicted upon him. With this interpretation of hell, it is unthinkable to imagine Christ being brought to such a place or reality. For if he went there, then, it means that he is still there continuing to pay the penalty forever. And then a question would come concerning our salvation, whether he accomplished it or not.

The idea of Christ having faced hell becomes worse when it is put together with another idea that suggests that sinners will not be consciously tormented forever, but will be annihilated. Annihilation is connected with a doctrine called 'Conditional Immortality'. According to this doctrine only the redeemed will have immortality conferred upon them as part of the experience of their salvation. And for moral reasons on the part of God, after death and judgement, all the wicked will be destroyed and cease to exist. The reason is that God is a God of love and not a sadist. God will not be delighted to see the creation being tormented forever.[4]

As the Church of England states it, annihilation seems to find roots among many theologians today. She states, "Annihilation might be a true picture of damnation than any of the traditional images of hell of eternal torments."[5] Now, with such an understanding of hell, with the idea claimed here that annihilation is the very right interpretation of hell, it becomes very difficult to think of him, being not only human but also God, 'Jesus - God and Man', as Pannenberg calls him, being annihilated. Therefore the affirmation that Christ's descent into hell signifies his lowest point of humiliation is disproved. This is also because, biblically, the lowest point in the state of the humiliation of Christ is not a descent into a local hell, but is the shameful death on the cross (cf. Philippians 2: 8).

4. Gray, "Destroyed for Ever," 14. Fuellenbach, *The Kingdom of God*, 107–110.

5. Graham and others, *The Mystery of Salvation:* 199.

CHRIST'S DESCENT AS HIS EXALTATION

The interpretation of Christ's descent to be the first stage in the state of his humiliation was first held by the Lutheran dogmaticians of the seventeenth century in opposition to the humiliation interpretation of the Reformed theologians. For the Lutherans the descent took place between his return to life in the grave and the resurrection.[6] That is, Jesus descended into hell before he was shown to be resurrected. For them the purpose of the descent was the proclamation of judgement by the Victor to the damned, and as such, it signified his triumph over hell.

The motive for this interpretation was probably to avoid the idea that it was Jesus' soul that went to the dead. For this would mean that he was not really dead. Hence they affirmed, "We simply believe that after the burial the entire person, God man, descended into hell . . ."[7] In this interpretation hell does not mean a local place in the underworld where souls of dead men are kept or being under guard by Satan. For it, hell is a final reality of the damned in which both evil men and Satan are kept. And therefore, when Christ went there after his resurrection (but before he showed himself to the world as risen from the dead), his aim was only to confirm his victory over all evils and the fact of their damnation.

One thing that is important about this interpretation of Jesus' descent into hell is its effort to avoid the notion that when a person dies it is only part of him (his body), that dies, and the soul continues to live. This is seen not only in the affirmation that it was the resurrected Christ who visited hell, but in its presupposition that men go directly to hell or heaven immediately after death. This, according to Braaten, was the belief of the Lutheran dogmaticians of the seventeenth century.[8] Thus, in this interpretation, the question of immortality of souls is explained away.

---

6. Pannenberg, *Jesus-God and Man,* 273; Cf. Stærk, "The Descent into Hell" (trans.), 22.

7. Tappert (ed.), *The Book of Concord,* 610

8. Braaten and Jenson (eds.), Christian *Dogmatics*. Volume 1, 548.

However, this interpretation has at least two problems; one exegetical, according to Pannenberg, and another Christological. For Pannenberg the interpretation of Christ's descent into hell to be the first point in the state of his exaltation is wrong because, while it claims to base its argument on the Petrine passages, it interprets them differently from what they mean. The passages do not suggest that the content of Jesus' preaching in hell was a pronouncement of doom by the Victor to the damned, as the exaltation interpretation claims to be the case.[9]

The Christological problem comes in because the interpretation claims that people go directly to heaven or hell immediately after death. This claim contradicts the fact that Jesus' resurrection presupposes or is the basis for the resurrection of all other people. For the idea conveyed in this claim is that the resurrection of other people is independent of the resurrection of Jesus.

Also, the claim that before Jesus' resurrection there were already people in heaven makes it impossible to speak of Christ as the first fruit of the resurrection as Paul does (1 Corinthians 15: 20–28). Likewise, the idea that there were some people already in hell, and others in heaven, during Christ's descent, seems to contradict the belief that Christ will be the principle executor of the final judgement after the general resurrection of the dead (cf. Matthew 25: 31–46). Therefore, the exaltation of Christ cannot be explained in terms of the descent into hell.

CONCLUSION

In concluding this chapter we affirm that the doctrine of Christ's descent into hell is not an appropriate expression of any of the two states of Christ. This means that it cannot be used to signify either of the states. Only two events do serve this purpose: the death on the cross is the lowest point in the state of the humiliation of Christ, and the resurrection is the first act in the state of his exaltation.

9. Pannenberg, Jesus-*God and Man*, 273.

5

The Doctrine of the Descent
in the Life of the Church in Africa

INTRODUCTION

IN THE PREVIOUS CHAPTER, we dealt with the question of states of Christ in relation to his descent into hell. We investigated the validity of the interpretation that Christ's descent was his humiliation and exaltation. We concluded that Christ's descent cannot either be humiliation nor exaltation because the former was complete once at the cross through his shameful suffering and death, and the later was fulfilled at his resurrection when he victoriously raised from the dead. The question that we are now going to deal with in this chapter concerns about the belief about Jesus' preaching in hell or to the dead. The aim is to consider its implication to Christian mission in an African context. Thus, the question we are considering here is the practical implications of the doctrine of Christ's descent into hell to Christian teaching and preaching within the context of the African church.

A POST-DEATH CHANCE FOR SALVATION

Let us first present the content in the belief that Christ preached in hell by considering the affirmation of MacCulloch who seems to stand for it with all his might. He strongly believes that it is possible for the souls beyond the grave to obtain forgiveness and to progress in knowledge and enlightenment. Because of this he likes the legend of Christ having left his cross erected in *hades* as having a profound truth, for it "is active in the other World as on this earth."[1]

Often it is a moral reason that is given in defence of the preaching to the dead. It is argued that Christ had to do so in order for him to have a just judgement in his execution of the last judgement.[2] The question of justice comes in because many generations lived and died before Christ's ministry on earth. These also needed to here the Gospel. Thus, for Braaten, here lies the theological significance of Christ's descent into hell; that in so far as we confess it "we are claiming that his work of salvation is universal and reaches beyond the limits of those who preach and hear the gospel."[3]

For Pannenberg this fact of a universalistic character of Christ's work of salvation brings a challenge to the church's understanding of itself in the midst of all humanity. For him salvation is not confined only to the one who consciously come into contact with the Gospel, for even "Jesus himself did not bind the promise of eschatological salvation to the full recognition of the significance of his own mission"[4] What is seen here is a gradual development of the concept of Christ's descent into hell from a simple affirmation of the preaching to the dead to the complex theological consideration of the self-understanding of Christianity.

Anyway, the concern here is not to discuss the question of who is the participant in the eschatological salvation. What we know is that we are commanded to preach the Gospel (Matthew 28: 19). In this context two lines of arguments will be considered.

1. MacCulloch, *The Harrowing of Hell,* 325
2. Cf. Stærk, "The Descent into Hell" (trans.), 40.
3. Braaten and Jenson (eds.), *Christian Dogmatics, Volume 1,* 549.
4. Pannenberg, *Jesus-God and Man,* 272.

The first one is that of preaching to those who lived before Jesus'
era and the second line is that which considers even those who
today have no chance to hear the Gospel before they die, or they
hear it, but not sufficiently enough to cause any effect.

First, the implication of the claimed necessity for Jesus to
preach also to those who lived before him is that God had kept a
closed eye to all generation that preceded Jesus. In other words, the
advocates of this idea want to portray a theory that before Christ
came to this world there was no gospel of any kind. However, according to the same texts which are claimed to speak of Christ's
descent, 1 Peter. 3:19, one finds that the history of God's work of
salvation does not begin with Jesus. For here, Noah is mentioned.
Through him God's message was delivered to the people.

Second, the argument which refers even to those who today
die without hearing the Gospel sounds very moral especially in view
of the fact that until today the Christian mission has not reached every quarter of the world and many are dying without being preached
to first. It is for this reason that Pannenberg feels that a consideration has to be made also to those who "only superficially come into
contact with the message of Christ."[5] However, here is a very big
practical problem in the life of the Church. What is suggested here is
a second chance for the dead to hear the Gospel. And then one may
ask if there is any necessity for believing before he dies.

Already there are some people today who feel no need for
believing before they die. According to the witness of one Indo-
nesian student of Fjellaug Mission School in Oslo, there are some
people in his country who are pleased with the idea that a Gospel
was preached in *hades*. For them this is good news for post-death
chance for salvation and which, therefore, allows them to lead
any life they want. In this case, as Reicke notes, "all responsibility
for behaviour in the earthly life is removed."[6] Here it is up to the
Church whether she will continue to retain this kind of belief of
Christ's preaching to the dead despite the dangerous implications
it gives to her people.

5. Pannenberg, *Jesus-God and Man*, 272.
6. Reicke, *The Disobedient Spirits*, 12.

THE AFRICAN ANCESTRAL CULT
UNCHALLENGED

The affirmation that Christ descended into hell, where he had a stay with the souls of dead men, is very good news to those who believe in ancestral spirits. Though the ancestral cult is a common phenomenon in Africa, according to MacCulloch, the belief that the dead are living in *hades* is not confined only to Africa, but it is universal. For example, the Eskimo are said to have some stories that tell about people who go to the dead to obtain boons or good luck, just as the Yoruba stories tell of young men who go to the land of the dead for the same purpose.

This universality of the living-dead might be the reason why the doctrine of Christ's descent into hell goes without being challenged today even among theologians. The only difference between African belief in ancestors and the belief of other societies is the fact that for the Africans, because of their unbroken sense of duty and respect to their elders, which continues beyond death, that belief extends up to the point of equating their ancestors with God as they venerate them. And in other contexts God is completely replaced by the ancestors, at least in people's understandings. This explains why in Africa there are a lot of sacrifices to the dead.[7]

Now let us suppose that it is to this kind of a people that the doctrine of Christ's descent into hell is taught. What would be their reaction? It is possible that whoever will be teaching them

7. MacCulloch, *The Harrowing of Hell*, 22. Also cf. Harton, *Patterns of Thought in Africa*, 21, 217; Mbiti, *African Philosophy and Religions*, 25, 58–63, etc. However, current researches affirm that sacrifices to ancestors done by Africans are offered to the Supreme God through ancestors as mediators (see for example Mligo, *Elements of African Traditional Religion*, 63–65; cf. Ilomo, *African Religion*, 10–14; cf. The prayer of the Bakossi to Ngoe the primeval ancestor in Sundermeir, *The Individual and Community*, 123–125) An example of African people who confuse God with ancestors in their understanding are the Kinga of Makete in Tanzania. Ilomo states: "Among the Kinga people in Tanzania, the term which corresponds to the English term 'forebears are *manguluve*. This term confuses some people, especially those who associate the term manguluve to Nguluve, God. For other people, the term *manguluve* seems to be the plural form of the term *nguluve*." (Ilomo, *African Religions*, 12, italics is in original).

might be pleased that his message is well received by them while, in fact, they have done so for reasons other than what he thinks. When the Christian mission comes to the believer in ancestors with its affirmation of Christ having once descended there, he will probably be happy with his message on the grounds that also his dead relative has or had the chance to hear the Gospel of Christ.

In any case, the fact that Jesus went to the dead confirms the belief in the living-dead (a term coined by Mbiti[8] and adopted by other scholars, e.g., Thorpe.[9]). And then, as is the case with Africans, a big problem will arise when the missionary asks them to stop offering sacrifices to them. What reason will satisfy them that their dead parents, as dead people, do not need anything from them according to Christian teaching while Christ himself so cared for the dead that he even went to offer them salvation in hell? This question is actually what makes Christian teaching about Jesus' selvific work difficult among African churches whose believers confuse about ancestors and Christ (God). Therefore dogmaticians like Stærk, who complain that the doctrine of Christ's descent into hell is not given its proper place in the Church, and because of that they would like to make it known even to the common person,[10] have to consider whether that 'common person', who sacrifices to ancestors will be helped to avoid religious syncretism by that understanding.[11]

SUPPORT FOR THE DOCTRINE OF PURGATORY

Both the doctrine of the descent and the doctrine of purgatory presuppose a continuation of life after death to a local hell or purgatory, respectively. Normally purgatory is differentiated from hell by the argument that while hell is the eschatological final fate of

---

8. Mbiti, *African Religions*, 75.

9. Thorpe, African *Traditional Religions*, 38.

10. Stærk, "The Descent into Hell" (trans.), p.1.

11. For the meaning of the concept of 'religious syncretism' see Gehman, *African Traditional Religion*, 270–283; Schreiter, *Constructing Local Theologies*, 144–158; Mugambi, *Christianity and African Culture*, 68–69.

the damned, purgatory is an intermediate state between hell and heaven.[12] However, this distinction is immaterial so long as both are taken to be places from which souls of dead people can be rescued, either by the descent of Christ[13] or through indulgences. Neither is it a permanent region of souls.[14]

Now we understand that one of the doctrines which were held as repugnant to the Reformers was the doctrine of purgatory. They detested the doctrine simply because it gave a wrong assurance of salvation to people. People were made to relay on the pope's power of keys; that through indulgences not only were souls delivered from purgatory, but also that, that was a way for making payment for sin which was committed.[15]

As MacCulloch seems to point out, it appears that the doctrine of purgatory developed directly out of the popular doctrine of the descent. While other religions portrayed heroes as having gone to rescue their beloved in hell, Christians began to talk about Jesus as their hero who went to hell. Later on the efficacy of prayer replaced the dramatic descent, in which case also Mary was believed to have had the power to alter the course of the fate of one's soul in purgatory.[16]

Together with the power of Mary, a question concerning the power of keys developed. Both of them are dealing with the same problem: To help the soul in purgatory to attain salvation. From this correlation of the two doctrines it would seem that to uphold the doctrine of the descent and criticise purgatory is a great contradiction.[17] Dogmatically they are either both sound doctrines or unsound. If, as the Church of England once stated, "the doctrine concerning purgatory, pardon, . . . is a fond (i.e. Foolish) thing, vainly invented and grounded upon no warranty of Scripture,

12. Cf. Braaten and Jenson (eds.), *Christian Dogmatics*, 548.

13. MacCulloch, *The Harrowing of Hell*, 253.

14. Cf. The description of 'hades', by Vines, *An Expository Dictionary of the New Testament* Sv. HADES

15. Tappert (ed.), *The Book of Concord*, 185.

16. Cf. MacCulloch, *The Harrowing of Hell*, 35.

17. Cf. Reicke, *The Disobedient Spirits*, 44.

but rather repugnant to the Word of God,"[18] so is the doctrine of Christ's descent into hell. For this, too, is not supported directly, but only by disputable Biblical references.[19]

CONCLUSION

This chapter dealt with the implication of the doctrine of the descent to the African church. It examined the correlation between the doctrine of the descent and African teachings and beliefs about ancestors and sacrifices. It has also surveyed the correlation between the church's teaching about the descent and the doctrine of purgatory as was repudiated by reformers. We have concluded in both observations that the doctrine of the descent clearly correlates with both doctrines: the doctrine of ancestral worship and the doctrine of purgatory. This correlation makes teaching and preaching difficult in African churches because they encourage religious syncretism among believers who would not like to jettison their African religious worships.

18. Noll (ed.) *Confessions and Catechisms,* 220.

19. Cf. Schwarz, *Responsible Faith,* 254.

6

The Godforsaken Interpretation

"Elo-i, Elo-i, la ma sabach-thani? . . .'My God, my God, why hast thou forsaken me?"

—MARK 15: 34

INTRODUCTION

IN THE PREVIOUS CHAPTER, we examined the danger which the doctrine of the descent poses to Christian teaching and preaching within the church in Africa. In this chapter, we make a brief survey of the way in which scholars struggle to redeem the doctrine from that malignant danger. We examine the interpretation of the doctrine of the descent in relation to the passion of Jesus. We focus on the words of Jesus on the cross: "My God, my God, why hast thou forsaken me?" that indicate his exclusion from God's nearness and God's siding with the worldly authorities in bringing a contradiction from what Jesus preached and lived. In this survey, therefore, we determine whether the alternative interpretation solves the danger or adds more problems to the life of the church.

THE PASSION OF JESUS AS HELL

Some scholars, such as Martin Luther, John Calvin, Helmut Thielicke, and Karl Barth, make the identification of hell in the suffering of Jesus. It is presupposed in one of the ninety-five theses of Luther, when he says, "Hell, purgatory, and heaven seem to differ the same as despair, fear, and assurance of salvation."[1] But in another context Luther explicitly relates Christ's descent into hell to his agony in Gethsemane that he calls the nadir of his humiliation.[2] For Calvin, too, whose interpretation is based on the words of Christ on the cross: My God, my God, why hast thou forsaken me? Christ's descent into hell means despair and distress into which he was cast.[3] Calvin's interpretation was followed by Barth who, in 1935, only five years after MacCulloch's defence of Christ's preaching to the dead as the content in the doctrine of the descent, delivered a number of lectures on the "Chief problems of dogmatics with references to the Apostles' Creed." For him the descent into hell has its reference from none other than Mark 15: 35, "My God, my God, why hast thou forsaken me."[4]

According to Barth the clause 'he descended into hell', does not stand in isolation from the preceding two clauses, 'crucified' and buried'. For him all the three present "very remarkable and extraordinary description of the death of Jesus of Nazareth,"[5] a description of the self surrender of 'God' to the state and fate of man. Even in countries like Norway where there is a strong tradition to link Jesus' descent with the preaching to the dead, still there are theologians, e.g., LØnning, who follow the 'godforsaken' (Moltmann's term[6]) interpretation.[7]

---

1. Noll, *Confessions and Catechisms*, 30

2. Moltmann, *The Trinity and the Kingdom*, 77

3. Barth, *The Faith of the Church*, 81

4. Barth, *Credo: A Presentation of the Chief Problems*, 88.

5. Barth, *Credo: A Presentation of the Chief Problems*, 38.

6. Moltmann, *The Crucified God*, 145.

7. Stærk, "The Descent into Hell" (trans.), 26.

This kind of interpretation is quite different from the literal interpretation that speaks of the preaching to the dead. Nor can it be compared with the Lutheran interpretation that speaks of the descent as the lowest point in the state of Christ's humiliation. For this, too, understands the descent literally and shows Jesus to have been in hell where he was tormented. The godforsaken interpretation, though like that of the Lutheran one which identifies hell in the real suffering of Christ, does not locate that suffering in the other world, but here on earth in the life of Jesus of Nazareth.

Helmut Thielicke sees the passion of Jesus as a separation from God in all its forms. For him, the passion of Jesus is "ultimate forsakenness."[8] According to Thielicke, a person can be in Hell while still here on earth. He affirms that "hell is simply a situation in which we must recognize God without being able to come to Him."[9]

Pannenberg and Moltmann, with almost similar arguments, explain why Jesus' passion is his descent into hell. For Pannenbrg Jesus' passion was hell because it was a contradiction of what he knew about the eschatological nearness of God which he himself had lived and preached. He felt that God was excluding him from that nearness. And because this happened in spite of this clear knowledge of God whom he knew was very clause to him, this fact is nothing else but hell.[10] Pannenberg does not see the painfulness of Jesus' death only just from the naked fact of the cross, that is, the mode of the execution and crucifixion. He sees it mostly in the entire course that led him to such death.

Jesus had preached the eschatological nearness of God as having come in his presence. His closeness to God was revealed not only in his words but also in his deeds. When he cast out demons, it was by the finger of God. He showed himself to be Zealous for the house of God, whom he called his Father, and that he and the Father were one. Jesus also claimed to give a proper interpretation of the law. All these claims were made invalid by his death.

8. Thielicke, *I believe*, 124.

9. Ibid., 127.

10. Pannenberg, *Jesus-God and Man*, 271.

Jesus' death brought to his not only physical pains but also mental. He died not only as condemned by the Romans, but also as one rejected by his own people in the name of the authority of the very God whom he called his Father. Apparently, God had vindicated the authorities that condemned him of blasphemy for his having identified himself with God. God seemed to denounce everything that Jesus had done and claimed. Thus for Jesus his death was not only a biological fact, but also meant an end of everything that he had lived for.[11]

The fact that Jesus' death brought a contradiction to the course he had set is substantiated with the behaviour of his disciples. Being shaken by his death they dispersed in despair. The whole group that had followed him disintegrated; no one was left to continue that work of his master. Even Peter went back to his former fishing occupation! (John 21: 4–7). Thanks for the resurrection that revived anew their faith in him. Otherwise, today the story could be different.

The apparent fact of God being on the side of the authorities which condemned Jesus is what makes Moltmann to describe Jesus as the 'godforsaken'. Like Pannenberg, For Moltmann we can understand the painfulness of Jesus' death not in the fact of his condemnation by the Jews and Romans, "but in relation to his God and Father, whose closeness and whose grace he himself had proclaimed."[12]

Really Jesus died the death of a sinner. For his death on the cross meant a complete exclusion from God's nearness which could be experienced only by a sinner. This was hell for him. However, for Moltmann, Jesus' abandonment and separation from his God and Father on the cross was something that took place within God himself. This argument is based on the fact that after Jesus' separation in death he was again raised through the glory of his Father. Thus he would say, "The cross of the Son divides God from God to the utmost degree of enmity and distinction. The resurrection

---

11. Ibid., 269.

12. Moltmann, *The Crucified God,* 146.

of the Son abandoned by God unites God with God in the most intimate fellowship."[13]

Hence, with Moltmann, we can say that the one who suffered on the cross was not only man but also God himself. And because of this, Jesus, as the Son of God, did not alone experience the painful situation in which he was brought. It must have affected all the persons in the Trinity. Therefore God suffered. God was crucified at the cross!

For Moltmann the explanation of other scholars that during Jesus' suffering "his divinity was for a short while concealed, that is, it did not exercise its power,"[14] would not be welcome. This is because it excludes God's involvement in this suffering. From this fact that God suffered, then, it is relevant for us to speak of what it cost him for our salvation. However, to state that God suffered is different from saying that he died. That is why, for Moltmann again, "Jesus 'death cannot be understood 'as the death of God', but only as death in God"[15] Therefore, the death of God and the death of Jesus in God are different. This is what also entails the two natures of Jesus: his mortal humanity and immortal divinity.

THE PROPRIETY OF THE 'GODFORSAKEN' INTERPRETATION

Biblically the interpretation which sees hell in the passion of Jesus is not alien. Figuratively, the fact that one may suffer while still alive is expressed in Numbers 16: 33 where men are consciously thrown in fire. And for Stærk Psalms. 22: 1 and 88: 66, together, support the meaning that the suffering of Jesus can be called his descent into hell.[16] Furthermore, the Bible differentiates two kinds of death, the death of the righteous and the death of the sinner. The former is common death, but the latter is not. The difference is first

13. *Ibid.,* 152.

14. Bath, *The faith of the church,* 80.

15. Moltmann, *The Crucified God,* 207.

16. Stærk, "The Descent into Hell" (trans.), 78.

seen in the manner of death itself (cf. Numbers 16: 29; 26: 10): The death of the righteous is preferred and prayed for (Numbers 23: 10), but that of the sinner is too disgraceful (cf. 1 Kings 22:23–39).

The second difference of the two deaths is the fact that the death of the sinner, figuratively brings one down into *hades* not to heaven. It is the righteous person who goes up to heaven, and his death is said to be a 'lifting' or 'taking up', as it is spoken of the death of Stephen (Acts 8:1, 20:20). The death of the wicked is thus a hell to him or her because it separates him or her from the sphere of God's love and nearness.

The 'godforsaken' interpretation thus identifies the death of Jesus as being the death of a wicked person just because it was not a fine death for him. In the language of Numbers 16: 33, Jesus was brought down into hell while alive. Here 'alive' means being consciously aware of the contradiction brought by his death. Jesus was made to have stood for the wrong cause and those who opposed him were made to be right. Thus for the 'godforsaken' interpretation a possibility to speak about Jesus bearing the sins of the world is opened. Here the theology of the cross finds its basis.

However, though the identification of Christ's descent with his passion is right dogmatically, it is doubtful whether it really takes into consideration the original meaning of the descent as it first appeared in the creed. According to the Sirmium or dated creed, in which the descent clause was first inserted, Jesus, having descended into hell, is said to have regulated the things there and because of his presence the gate keepers of hell shuddered.

In fact, it would appear that anyone reading or reciting the Apostles' Creed, when he comes to this part, the first impression he gets from it does not go very far from the fact that Christ went to the realm of the dead after his death. Even the order of words reveals this fact: "He was crucified; died and buried: he descended into hell." Thus the 'godforsaken' interpretation comes from this simple idea that Christ literally descended into a local place of the dead. The reason for doing so is well understood from what is already discussed in the preceding chapters. It satisfactorily avoids all the dogmatical and practical problems that are involved in all other interpretations of the descent.

However, if the sole aim of the godforsaken' interpretation is to conceal the misleading literal interpretation of the descent, then it still has the task of doing so. Its advocates have to look at the way that all Christians can understand this good interpretation of theirs. For it appears that this interpretation of the descent can be understood well by scholars and not so much by the majority common people.

CONCLUSION

This chapter has attempted to discuss an alternative interpretation of the descent doctrine to try concealing its malignant interpretations discussed in the previous chapters. The doctrine has been interpreted in terms of the passion of Jesus. The words of Jesus on the cross: "My God, my God, why hast thou forsaken me?" have been the focus. Jesus' exclusion from the nearness of God and God's siding with the worldly authorities in bringing vivid the contradiction from what Jesus preached and lived was hell to him. This is because only a sinner could experience that situation. Jesus experienced hell in order to save humanity. However, according to the above discussion, this interpretation cannot be deemed satisfactory because only theologians can understand. In that case, the interpretation still leaves a task to its adherents to make it understood to majority common people that comprise the church.

7

Concluding Remarks

IN VIEW OF THE above discussion one may still ask if the clause about Christ's descent into hell is a legitimate expression of the Christian faith at all. Should the Apostles' Creed continue to exhibit this controversial clause? What has been noted by this study is that the doctrine of the descent into hell cannot be claimed to be Apostolic. This is because it presupposes the immortality of souls, a doctrine that is neither in the New Testament nor in the Christian teachings.

MacCulloch concluded his discussion on the doctrine of the descent with an appeal to the mass that the article of the descent should not be taken away from the Creed before considering its popularity in showing the instinctive belief in God's love beyond the grave.[1] MacCulloch's appeal reveals that since his time the presence of the descent doctrine in the Creed has been questioned. Its presence in the Creed might not have caused problems to the people at the time of its inception because it expressed their common belief about the 'living-dead' that, as seen from MacCulloch's presentation, is universal.

However, later on we see theologians beginning to have some doubts concerning it. They found out that it was not contained in

1. MacCulloch, *The Harrowing of hell*, 326.

the early Christian creedal formula, but was only a late Western insertion. Lane calls it "one of the principle innovations,"[2] and Kelly describes it as a substance that was "added to the second article of the creed, and which involves exegetical difficulties of no mean order."[3] No one will deny Kelly's affirmation that it is difficult to interpret the clause. The interpretations given to it in this study confirm the fact.

While Lane and Kelly speak only of its peculiarity, theologians of the Augsburg Confession warn people from making disputations and speculations concerning it. They want believers to 'swallow' the descent as a pill without questioning it. The question expressed in the clause, for the majority, is simple: After death Christ descended into the realm of the dead. From this simple affirmation, a lot of explanations on the how and when of the descent are given. For others Christ's descent affirms his death; that he, as human being, really died. This becomes an affirmation of his humanity.

However, this claim that the descent affirms the humanity of Jesus is disproved by the fact that the motives for the insertion of the descent clause in the creed were not polemical. None during Jesus' earthly ministry ever doubted Jesus was not a real man. On the contrary, he was accused of pretending to be someone other than a mere man. His identification with God was, according to his contemporaries, a blasphemy. And therefore they killed him.

Some go further. With the help of verses from 1 Peter 3: 19 and 4: 6, they describe Jesus' descent as having entailed an active stay in the realm of the dead; that he preached to them, and had a final victory over Satan. The belief of the preaching to the dead then is further interpreted theologically as signifying the universality of the salvific work of Christ. In this case Christianity is said to be challenged about its self-understanding in the midst of all humanity. The idea contained in this challenge is that the participants in the eschatological salvation of God are not necessarily only those who have access to the Gospel during their earthly life, but also those who died in sin.

2. Link, *The Roots of Our Common Faith*, 99.
3. Kelly, *Early Christian Creeds*, 378.

Here, though the challenge brought to the Church concerning its self-identity may be valid, the basis of the challenge that the dead are preached to or will be preached to becomes not only awkward, but also very dangerous to the whole life of the Church, especially the church in African context of ancestral cults . For here, a post-death chance for salvation is evidently suggested. In this case no necessity for preaching or doing mission and believing during one's life is needed.

Others interpret Christ's descent into hell in terms of the two states of Christ. For them it is the lowest point in the humiliation of Christ in which he was physically tormented in hell. This interpretation, however, brings a problem in the understanding of Christ if he was divine at all. For, as hell is an eschatological reality of the separation forever of the damned from the love of God, the idea of Christ being separated forever from his Father becomes repugnant to faith.

Others identify Christ's descent as the first act in the state of his exaltation that happened between his return to life in the tomb and his resurrection. This interpretation, however, presupposes that some people were already in heaven and others in hell before Jesus' death and resurrection. In this case, this interpretation goes against the Christian belief that Christ is the first fruit of the resurrection and the principle executor of the final judgement.

Another interpretation denies all the literal interpretations of the descent that speak of Christ having gone to hell, whether to preach or to be tormented. This interpretation understands the clause as signifying his passion and death. For this interpretation, Christ's death presented a great contradiction to his earthly mission and understanding of his Father. In his death Jesus felt to be forsaken by his God and completely excluded from the nearness of God that he had himself lived and preached. For him this was hell; it brought to him both physical and mental pain.

However, though this interpretation is dogmatically safe, it has two problems. The first one is its exegetical negligence. It fails to take into account the original meaning of the descent as it first appeared in the Creed. There, something more than passion was meant. From the very beginning a functional purpose of the descent was mentioned: Christ regulated the things in hell.

The second problem is practical. For many people, the clause of the descent is understood very literally: Christ descended into hell after death; not before! The order of words of the Creed supports their understanding. Thus, the practical question is how are these people going to be helped to clear away the wrong conception they had for so long time, especially if nothing will be done to the Creed itself?

It would seem that the Church today has only two alternatives: Either to let her people continue professing Christ's descent into hell regardless of the many, and sometimes awkward, implications it gives; or be courageous and decide to delete it from the Creed. Maybe, the question to ask here should be the following: What will be the cost if the latter alternative is taken?

It seems to us that the Apostles' Creed will hardly be affected by the deletion of the descent clause from it. All the Christological affirmations can be done without the descent clause take for example the question of the universal salvation which is claimed to be expressed by the descent of Christ into hell. This universal salvation can be affirmed without the doctrine of the descent. And, in fact, it cannot be explained in terms of Jesus' descent into hell and the preaching to the dead, whether the descent and the preaching are taken literally or figuratively. This is simply because no theology can be developed out of hell (from the dead), but only in the life, work, death (Cross) and the resurrection of Jesus Christ.

The descent clause is probably not an appropriate expression of the Christian faith because, as it has already been seen, it does not have a single meaning that can be held by all Christians. And then, it becomes more problematic and dangerous when others interpret it as offering an assurance for having another chance to hear the Gospel in hell. Also the affirmation that Jesus went to preach to the dead is a very strong support for the ancestral cult, especially to those societies, mostly African, in which the belief in the living-dead is still strong. The descent doctrine confirms that people do not really die, which is the very strong presupposition used in the veneration of ancestors.[4]

Thus, in order for the Christian mission to be effective in such societies, and to teach them, "You shall not have other gods besides me," it is proper to think if there is any place for the doctrine of the descent. As far as we understand, it will not be possible to convince the African traditionalist to stop from making sacrifices of bulls to his dead parents if at the same time he is told that after death Jesus went to live and work among the dead in the under-world.

Thus from this analysis of the different interpretations and implications of the doctrine of Christ's descent into hell, it is found that the role played by the descent clause in the Apostles' Creed is not only insignificant to Christology, but also dangerous to the practical side of the Church. This means, therefore, that something has to be done concerning it. If there are people who would wish it to be taken out of the Creed, we are among them!

4. Africans believe that when a person dies, the spirit separates from the body and joins other spirits. However, the identity of this spirit remains the same as the one which the person had before death. For Africans this means that death is a continuation of life from normal human life to spiritual life in the spirit world (see Mbiti, *Introduction to African Religion*, 122–126; Mbiti, *African Religions and Philosophy*, 83–91; Magesa, *African Religion*, 52; Gehman, *African Traditional Religion*, 138–143; Mugambi, *Christianity and African Culture*, 202–203).

Bibliography

Barth, Karl. *Credo: A Presentation of the Chief Problems of Dogmatics with Reference to the Apostles' Creed*. London: Hodder & Stoughton, 1936.

———. *The Faith of the Church: A Commentary on the Apostles' Creed*. London: Collins, 1960.

Black, Matthew (ed.). *Peake's Commentary on the Bible*. London: Thomas Nelson and Sons, 1962.

Braaten, Carl and Robert W. Jenson (eds.). *Christian Dogmatics*, Volume 1 & 2. Philadelphia: Fortress Press, 1984.

Clowney, Edmund P. *The Message of 1 Peter*. Illinois: Inter-Varsity Press, 1988.

Cowen, Tyler and Robin Hanson. "Are Disagreements Honest? (2001). Online: hanson.gmu.ed/deceive.pdf.

Fish, Stanley. *Is There a Text in this Class? The Authority of Interpretive Communities*. Cambridge, Massachusetts & London, England: Harvard University Press, 1980.

Fuellenbach, John. *The Kingdom of God: The Message of Jesus Today*. Maryknoll, New York: Orbis Books, 1995.

Gehman, Richard. *African Traditional Religion in Biblical Perspective*. Kijabe Kenya: Kijabe Printing Press, 1989.

Graham, Alec and others. *The Mystery of Salvation: The Story of God's Gift*. A Report by the Doctrine Commission of the General Synod of the Church of England. London: Church House Publishing, 1995.

Gray, Tony. "Destroyed for Ever: An Examination of the Debates Concerning Annihilation and Conditional Immortality." *Themelios* 21: 2 (1996): 14–18.

Harton, Robin. *Patterns of Thought in Africa and the West*. London: Cambridge University Press, 1993.

Ilomo, Farles Ipyana. *African Religion: A Basis for Interfaith Dialogue Today*. Dar es Salaam: University of Dar es Salaam Press, 2013.

Kelly, J. N. D. *Early Christian Creeds*. London: Longman, 1972.

Kittel, Gerhard and Gerhard Friedrich (eds.) *Theological Dictionary of the New Testament*, Abridged in One Volume. Grand Rapids, Michigan: William B. Eerdmans, 1985.

Lenski, R. C. H. *The Interpretation of I and II Epistles of Peter, the Three Epistles of John and the Epistle of Jude*. Minneapolis: Augsburg, 1966.

Link, Hans-Georg. *The Roots of Our Common Faith: Faith in the Scriptures and in the Early Church*. Geneva: World Council of Churches, 1984.

MacCulloch, J. A. *The Harrowing of Hell: A Comparative Study of an Early Christian Doctrine*. T & T Clark, 1930.

Magesa, Laurenti. *African Religion: The Moral Traditions of abundant Life*. Nairobi: Paulines Publications Africa, 1997.

Mbiti, John S. *African Religions and Philosophy*. Nairobi: Heinemann, 1969.

———. *Introduction to African Religion*. Second Edition. Nairobi, Kenya: East African Educational Publishers, 1991.

Mligo, Elia Shabani. *Elements of African Traditional Religion*. Eugene, Oregon: Wipf and Stock, Resource Publications, 2013.

———. *Symbolic Interactionism in the Gospel according to John: A Contextual Study on the Symbolism of Water*. Eugene, Oregon: Wipf and Stock, 2014.

Moltmann, Jörgen. *The Crucified God*. London: SCM Press, 1974.

———. *The Trinity and the Kingdom of God*. London: SCM Press, 1981.

Mugambi, J.N.K. *Christianity and African Culture*. Nairobi, Kenya: Acton Publishers, 2002.

Noll, Mark A. (ed.) *Confessions and Catechisms of the Reformation*. Baker Book House, 1991.

Pannenberg, Wolfhart. *Jesus-God and Man* London: SCM Press, 1968.

———*What is Man?: Contemporary Anthropology in Theological Perspective*. Philadelphia: Fortress Press, 1970.

Pfeiffer, Charles F. And Everett F. Harrison (eds.). *The Wycliffe Bible Commentary*. Chicago: Mody Press, 1962.

Reicke, Bo. *The Disobedient Spirits and Christian Baptism: A Study of 1 Pet. III. 19 and Its Context*. Lund: Häkan Ohlsoons Boktryckeri, 1946.

Reinecker, Fritz. *A Linguistic Key to the Greek New Testament*. Grand Rapids, Michigan: Zondervan, 1980.

Schaff, Philip and Henry Wace (eds.). *A Select Library of Nicene and Post-Nicene Fathers of Christian Church*. Volume IV. Edinburgh: T. & T., Clark, 1987.

Schreiter, Robert. *Constructing Local Theologies*. Maryknoll, New York: Orbis Books, 1985.

Schwartz, Hans. *Responsible Faith: Christian Theology in the Light of 20th-Century Questions*. Minneapolis: Augsburg, 1986.

Stærk, Rolf E. "The Descent into Hell" (trans.). A Thesis Submitted to the Norwegian Lutheran School of Theology. Oslo, Norway, 1994.

Sundermeier, Theo. *The Individual and Community in African Traditional Religions*. Hamburg: LIT Verlag, 1998.

Tappert, Theodore (ed.). *The Book of Concord: The Confessions of the Evangelical Lutheran Church*. Philadelphia: Fortress Press, 1981.

Thielicke, Helmut. *I believe: the Christians' Creed*. Philadelphia: Fortress, 1965.

Thorpe, S. A. *African Traditional Religions: An Introduction*. Pretoria: University of South Africa, 1991.

Vine, W. E. *Expository Dictionary of New Testament Words*. London: Oliphants, 1969.